Merry
Christmas
Mike!

from
Gabor
1990

ACKNOWLEDGMENTS

We thank all the people who helped us in the difficult task of writing, photographing and filming this story, with special thanks to: His Majesty the King of Thailand and the Royal Thai Government and Tourist Authority of Thailand; Mr Apichat, Mrs Amporn and Kata, Noi and Boomsong, Amin, Ip, Sahat, Em and all the nest gatherers who understood the importance of recording their tradition; *National Geographic* magazine, especially Bill Garrett, Charles McCarry, Bob Poole, Al Royce, Tom Kennedy, Kent Kobersteen, Bruce McElfresh, Larry Kinney, George Von Kantor and all the staff, for their advice, encouragement and support; Raymond DeMoulin, general manager of the Professional Photography Division and vice-president of Eastman Kodak Company, for his belief and support from the beginning of the project, Dr James E. Patton, manager, Manufacturing Materials and Development, Charles M. Weller, assistant to manager, Manufacture and Materials, and all the other members of the Professional Photography Division at Kodak who made the impossible task of photographing in the caves possible; Monsieur Pierre Rietzler, president of Leica (France), Monsieur Yves Maxence, Herr Hans Zurcher, Madame Janus and all the Leica team for their generous assistance; Thai Airways, especially Mr Prajak Jamrusmechoti for his enthusiasm and co-operation; Mr Suwan and Captain Philippe Cathala of the *June Hong Chian Lee*; Chino and Elizabeth; Sylvain Bardoux, whose skills helped us to capture the world of the nest gatherers; Marie-France and Jacques-Yves de Rorthay, Michel Tallard and all of the 'Au Vieux Campeur' team; Mr Jo Daguenet, director of Edelrid (France), for his generosity; Warren and Tuê Blake; Dr Kong of the Chinese University of Hong Kong, Dr Kang Nee of the National University of Singapore, Dr Memie Kwok; Pictorial, especially Pierre and Eddy Gassmann, Christian, Martine and Fred, who brought about wonders behind his machine, and all the team; Robert and Cathy Auclerc and Christine de Cherisey for their help; and finally Benoît Nacci, art director of Nathan, for his creativity and imagination.

TECHNICAL INFORMATION

Photographing inside the caves was a highly technical challenge. The large flashes needed for shooting in such vast, dark caverns had to be avoided because they would have disturbed the thousands of swiftlets nesting there. Kodak Ektapress Gold 400 and 1600 professional film allowed us to keep saturated colours in the highlights while bringing out details hidden in the deep shadows.

All the photographs were taken with Leica R5, R6 and M6. Despite the tricky light conditions, the cameras were extremely accurate and withstood the dirt and humidity, as they had done for *Honey Hunters of Nepal*.

All the prints used in this book were made by Pictorial, Paris.

To Sara
and
the men who go where the
birds fly

First published in Great Britain in 1990 by
Thames and Hudson Ltd, London

Printed and bound in Italy

Stalactites and rocks eroded into pointed teeth guard the entrance to Rimau Cave, the Malay word for tiger. Inside, shadows veil a cavern as large as a cathedral. The twittering of thousands of birds echoes from distant recesses. From the cave floor bamboos bleached white with age rise fused together in pylons. From these foundations other bamboos soar ninety metres high, woven to the cave walls like a huge spiderweb. The bizarre scaffolding of flimsy bamboos and tangled vines seems inspired by a surrealistic dream.

Outside the cave, scores of rocky islets shimmer in a blue haze. In the distance the south-western coast of Thailand lies like a sleeping giant. Here on the archipelago of Phang-nga in the Andaman Sea, generations of men have travelled from island to island, passing from blue ocean to black rocks, from brilliant sunshine to dark caves in search of the edible nests of tiny birds, *Aerodramus fuciphagus* (the white-nest swiftlet) and *Aerodramus maximus* (the black-nest swiftlet). Vast caverns and narrow tunnels deep inside weather-worn islands are home to these birds who fly in the dark. The nests, made from the birds' saliva, are blended with chicken stock to produce the famous Chinese delicacy, bird's nest soup. Today the nests fetch US $2000 a kilo in Hong Kong. For hundreds of years men have gathered the 'white gold' of the caves. To nest gatherers like Sahat, Ip and Em, scaling the giant bamboo scaffolding is just another day's work. From a rickety bamboo perch Ip looks down into a well of darkness. Ninety metres below, a pool of daylight illuminates the cave floor. People, mere pinpricks, move about in a world that he left only thirty minutes before. There is nothing between his bare feet and the abyss but a few bamboo poles. His slightest error of judgment would be fatal. Yet, despite the danger, Ip is calm and sure of himself. He takes hold of a long vine and climbs with the effortless grace of a cat. Sahat follows, clenching a flaming torch between his teeth.

Em, the twenty-year-old apprentice, stands at the foot of a bamboo pylon watching the burning torches of Ip and his father, Sahat, flicker high above him until they are no more than distant stars on a black sky. Em and his teachers believe that gods inhabit this realm. The spirits of the cave, the bamboos and vines are fathers to them and must be treated with respect. Before climbing, the men ask the gods' permission to enter their domain. Failure to do so would mean a difficult and dangerous climb. Em places offerings of tobacco and incense at the foot of the pillar and murmurs a prayer: 'Gods of the pillar, please accept our gifts. Open the way of your bamboos!'

At the back of the cavern a large stalagmite symbolizes Tok Rimau, the god of the cave. Centuries of sacrifice and worship have instilled Rimau Cave with a hallowed presence. It is a world inhabited by gods, demons and the ghosts of men who have fallen from the bamboos. Spectral eyes seem to watch from all around.

Em rubs dry his clammy palms with guano. With his arms outstretched, he grabs hold of the bamboo pylon and, keeping his feet flat, he starts to climb. Reaching the top of the pillar, he enters a chamber. His feet sink into a thick carpet of guano seething with cockroaches. The smell of ammonia is almost overpowering. Leaving behind the safety of the rocks, Em takes hold of another bamboo pillar and continues to climb towards his masters.

The bamboos groan under Em's weight. His bare feet slip. In places the rock bulges over the bamboos like a

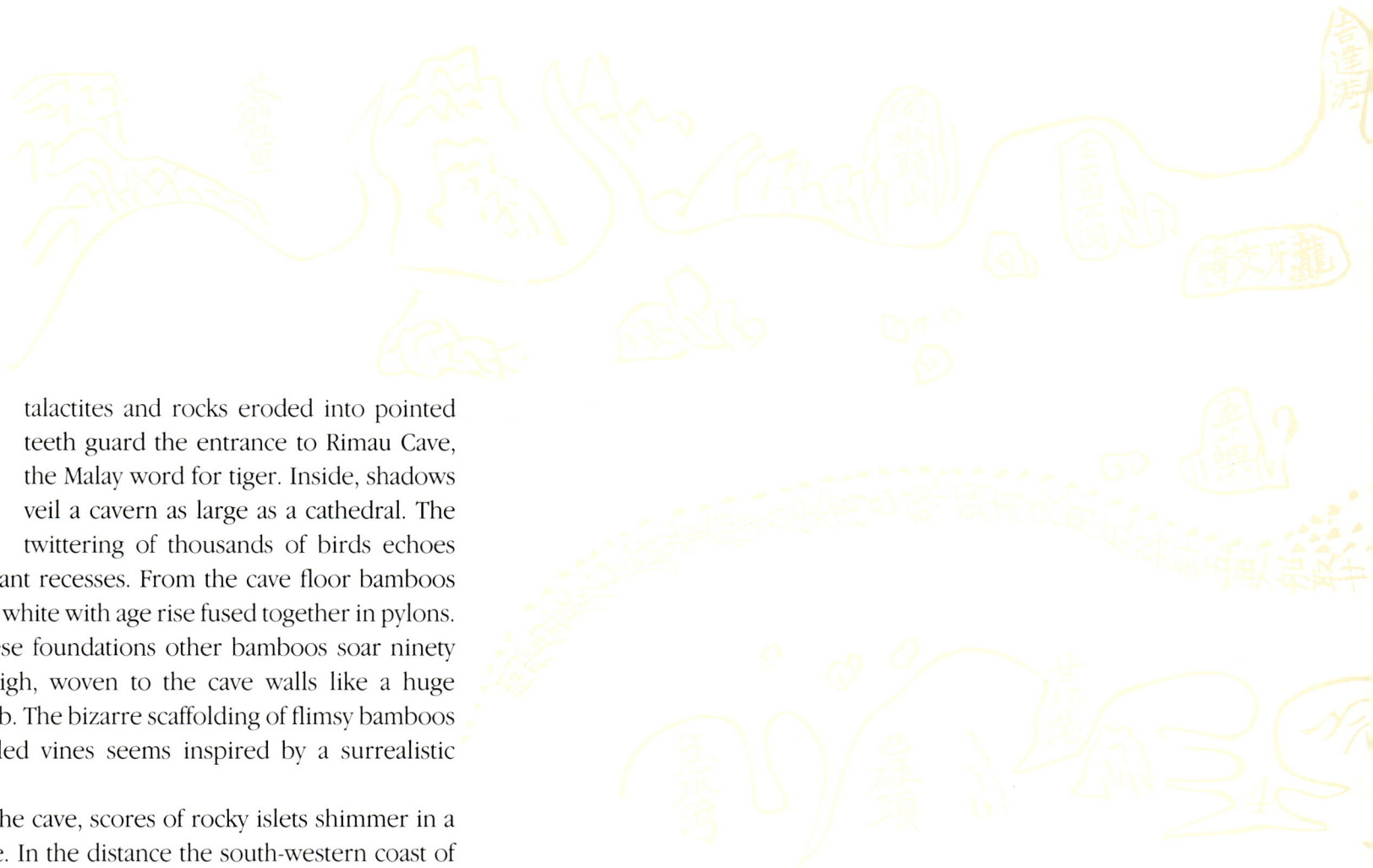

paunch, forcing him to step out over the abyss. Then he is climbing again over a bamboo span inclined at a 45 degree angle. Em crawls into a niche in the rock to rest, curling himself into a ball. Pearls of sweat run down his naked chest. The climb has not been easy for him. Ahead, Sahat and Ip are securing a narrow bridge across the cavern with vines. Em is relieved to find his teachers; their calm reassures him.

Although Sahat is fifty-five years old and silver-haired, he has the lean and muscular body of a much younger man. As he works, muscles ripple under tightly moulded skin. A white goatee beard, carefully trimmed to a point, makes him look like a wizard. A private, introspective man, he is most at ease when left alone in his cave.

Ip and Sahat have been climbing companions for the last thirty years. Their skill and close relationship allows them to climb where none of the others dares to venture. The two men dress in the same way, wearing a length of cotton material folded into their shorts and a small turban. A long chrome flashlight, hung across their bare chests, is used for emergencies or for scouring the vaults for nests. But there the similarity ends. Ip, fifteen years younger than his partner, has an open, good-natured face, curly black hair and handsome dark eyes. His sense of humour and boyish high spirits have won him many friends among the other nest gatherers. His amusing stories and comic impersonations have everyone in fits of laughter. Yet, despite his love of playing the fool, Ip is respected by Sahat and the others for his skill as a climber and for his knowledge of the caves.

The bamboos shudder under Em's awkward advance as he approaches Sahat and Ip. He does not yet possess the lithe step of his masters.

'Climb softly like a caress,' Ip whispers to Em as he goes to cross the bridge. 'We must be kind to the bamboos and vines that support us.'

As nimble as cats on a rooftop, Sahat and Ip traverse the void and disappear between immense stalactites that stand like ghostly white sentinels to the inner sanctuary of the cave. It is only when Em hears the cry 'Ma!' ('Come!') that he takes a deep breath and follows. Instinctively he asks Tok Rimau to let him pass safely. Ahead, Ip turns round to throw him a reassuring glance. Em steps forward. The bamboos bend under his weight. In the gloom he bangs his head against a long stalactite. A low booming sound reverberates slowly, echoing in the cave below, a solemn note like the call of the spirits from their hidden depths. A light flashes between the stalactites. A hand, invisible in the dark, takes Em's and leads him to the safety of the stalactites. This is as far as he would go.

Ip and Sahat tie vines that they have carried with them end to end, making a twenty-metre-long rope. Working by the red glow of their torches, the two companions search a large tangle of vines that lie wedged between an ivory stalactite and the wall of the cave until they find a place to which they can attach the rope. Sahat calls the knot of vines Hua Dao, a sacred place inhabited by the gods. Lianas used to secure the bamboo edifice hang down from it like dishevelled strands of hair. The nest gatherers never cut the old he must descend immediately, for it is a sign from the gods that it is dangerous for him to climb on the bamboos that day.

As Em waits for his companions to return, he prises off a nest. Its delicate white form fits neatly into the palm of his hand. He holds the nest up to the torchlight. It is translucent and woven with fine white filaments. The swiftlet regurgitates saliva in a long thin string which it weaves against the rock face. The saliva bonds quickly and strongly. Occasionally the nest gatherers find a swiftlet who has died a prisoner of its own making – its claws or feathers caught by a strand of the cement-fast saliva. Although the nest is virtually tasteless, Em eats it all. The climbers swear by its rejuvenating power. During the collecting season from February to July, they ascend the bamboo web at sunrise and descend only in the evening. Travelling light, without food or water, their sole source of nourishment comes from the nests, which they believe give them the energy of the birds. 'The nests give us strength and vitality. Our bodies can work harder and for much longer, just like these little birds who fly without ever landing.'

The nests are collected three times in a season. The birds rebuild them, usually in the same location. The first two nests are taken before the eggs are laid. The third nest is left for the birds to lay their eggs and raise their young. After the fledglings leave, the nest is removed, and the collectors return to their other occupations – Ip is a boat carpenter, Sahat and Em are fishermen.

Sahat and Ip return, their bags swollen with nests. Silently they move through galleries that honeycomb the cave. Without warning Ip shines his flashlight on the ceiling and shouts. The birds take off in fright and Ip searches the intricate rock folds for more of the 'white gold'. Startled swiftlets brush against the men. The beating of wings and clicking call are the only sounds in an otherwise still universe. Edible-nest swiftlets have the rare ability of navigating in the dark. Uttering a rattle call, they can find their way by echolocation, a system of acoustic orientation. This allows them to feed in distant localities by day, and return to roost late at night in caves and tunnels, far away from most predators.

The men climb higher, holding their burning torches

ones, in the belief that they were tied there by the magic of their forefathers. Sahat and Ip slide down the rope into the void.

Em watches their shadowy figures land on a platform that looks even lighter than the bamboos that had brought him here. The scratching of metal on rock is the only sound to reveal that men have entered the realm of the birds. From time to time their arms stretch upwards to a cluster of nests. Using a *rada*, a small, three-pronged iron fork, the men scrape the nests away from the wall of the cave. The nests are glued firmly to the rock by the birds' saliva which bonds like cement. The nest gatherers always use the *radas* of their ancestors to remove the nests. These irreplaceable tools are believed to possess magical powers. Pulling the nests away with their bare hands would be like stealing from the gods and would anger them. If a climber finds that he has forgotten his *rada*, between their teeth. The smell of burning resin pervades the air. Bats' eyes gleam. The shadows of the creeping men dance over the rippled folds of stalactites. Ip's torch burns low and he scratches the blackened tip against the cavern wall. Red sparks fall into the black void and the fire breathes again. Close to the roof of the chamber Ip sees the faint gleam of nests. To reach them he must crawl through a narrow gallery. It is difficult to get a grip on the rocks slippery with thick black slime. 'The rock is sweating,' he murmurs.

The spindly ribs of bamboos and vines lead to places that seem beyond the normal reach of man. But how did the nest gatherers defy the laws of gravity to weave a web that allows them to go where the birds fly? Sahat knows the legend of their ancestors.

'The first people to inhabit these islands came from the southern province of Satun. Their leader, a sage called Tok Ta Pa, knew how to deal with the spirits. He could climb where no man had ever been before. Working alone, he built the *né tong* (the intestines).'

According to Sahat, each time this ancient hammered a bamboo pole into the rock, he called upon the spirits for protection. He instructed his companions waiting below not to utter a word, even if they saw him almost fall, for the demons might hear them and push him over.

Tok Ta Pa's magical powers earned him a nickname. One of his men rushed into camp with an urgent message one day. A nest gatherer had fallen. Though he had grabbed on to a stalactite, he would not be able to hold on for much longer. Tok Ta Pa must come quickly to save him. Much to the messenger's surprise, the sage calmly knocked three times on a rock and went back to cooking his meal of sticky rice. The man was anxious for his friend's safety and asked the wise man to hurry.

'Don't worry,' Tok Ta Pa reassured him. 'We have time to eat together.'

When they reached the cave a few hours later, the nest gatherer was calm despite his precarious position.

'How do you feel up there?' shouted Tok Ta Pa.

'Pretty comfortable,' the climber yelled back. 'While you were away I suddenly felt as if I was on the ground.'

Tok Ta Pa and the messenger built a bamboo scaffolding to bring him down. Tok Ta Pa was thereafter called 'Sticky Rice'.

'There was magic in those days and knowledgeable men like Tok Ta Pa had great powers,' says Sahat. 'Our ancestors could cross a void without the help of the bamboos, could see in the dark without a torch and enlist the help of the spirits. But nowadays the magic is lost. People like Tok Ta Pa no longer exist. We had better build our bamboos strong, for there is still a multitude of spirits living in the caves.'

Ip laughs at the older man's stories. 'Our people built the *né tong* with their brains,' he says.

'How could they have ever got up there without the help of the gods!' Sahat snaps, offended by this blasphemy.

Nowadays the nest gatherers are divided into two schools of thinking: the old beliefs of Sahat and the rational approach of Ip. For the younger man, the length of a man's life can be judged only by the way he maintains the bamboos. But theirs is a dangerous job and believer and sceptic alike take no chances. Every year, before the harvest begins, they sacrifice a buffalo to placate the gods. They believe that the gods will then be satisfied by the offering of blood and will not demand a man's life. The men have a special vocabulary for use inside the cave, as if it is, indeed, the gods' domain. Words like 'falling', 'slipping', 'death', 'blood' and 'fear' are never spoken there. They think that if the spirits hear such powerful words, they will be tempted to cause an accident.

On the bamboos the nest gatherers show no fear. The void does not seem to exist for them. There is never any talk of the danger that they face every day. Every man works with an ease born from having mastery over fear.

'My friends tell me, "You have a dangerous job, you could fall down easily," ' Sahat says. 'But that's not true; otherwise we would all be dead. My father fell three times but never died. It was not his time. Those who have committed bad deeds are the ones who die.'

But as Em follows his father on the bamboos, he remembers Ip's more practical advice: 'Leave your worries at the foot of the bamboo. Up there, think only of yourself and what you must do. Many have died by having thoughts of other things.'

The climbers concentrate on each step, moving calmly. The strength of the next bamboo is the key to survival. Some poles are so old that they crumble to dust. Men have died trusting a rotten bamboo.

'Tap the bamboo,' the men say. 'If it answers like cardboard, leave it. It has lost its strength. If it sings well, give it your weight. Never take just one vine, always take three or four.'

The collectors' determination to find the nests leads them into many dangerous situations. In one cave the birds enter through passages high in the cliff that lie inaccessible to man. The mouth of the cave is submerged by the sea. The only way for the nest gatherers to enter is to swim underwater. Another cave is accessible only by the smallest collectors. Holding their breath, they slide through a narrow shaft that opens into the top of a chamber two hundred metres high. No wonder that the passage is called Rapo ('Born a Second Time'). Where the rocks are too wet and the scaffolding rots quickly, the climbers have used their ingenuity to make a 'walking bamboo'. Like the lookout perched on top of a ship's mast, one man sits on a

The map running through the text is that of the famous Chinese admiral Cheng Ho (Zeng He). Between 1405 and 1433 he led seven maritime expeditions in voyages of exploration and in search of new items of trade. Some authorities credit him with the introduction of foreign nests into China.

fifteen-metre-long bamboo in a 'crow's nest', two crossed bamboos guyed by vines to the cave floor. From there he removes the nests and, when he is finished, he signals to his companions waiting below to move the walking bamboo to the next wall.

The men's torches burn low. Each of them carries three for the day's work. When only a half remains, they know it is time for them to meet and commence the long descent. It is sunset when they reach the cave floor. Inside the tomb of rock they have passed the day cut off from the outside world. They do not know if it has been stormy or if it was another ferociously hot day. They hang their bags filled with nests on a high beam. Their dark skin is smeared with dirt. One by one they walk into the sea to wash. They return and cover their faces with talcum powder. Their ghostly white faces stare vacantly out to the sea. The sun, a giant red ball on the horizon, slowly disappears. As the sunset fades, an explosion of birds fills the sky. Far above, a hawk glides large, bold and slow, waiting for an opportunity to swoop down on the birds. Hundreds of swiftlets arriving from distant feeding grounds dart into the cave to roost for the night, while bats fly out to begin their nocturnal wanderings.

The throbbing of a motor rouses Ip. He recognizes Ron, the chief nest gatherer of a nearby cave, and with a wave of his hand beckons to him. His motor stops and the open wooden barque bobs against the cave jetty. The lapping of the sea and the piercing cries of the birds fill the silence. In the fading light the men quickly unload the boat filled with giant bamboos and vines brought to repair the web and enter the camp.

Located at the mouth of the cavern, the camp is made entirely of bamboo: walls, floors and partitions. A loosely woven platform, suspended by lianas to stalactites, juts out from the cave entrance over the sea. Each man has a separate sleeping area of his own, partitioned by a light screen. A pin-up girl is the only female in this all-male camp. Women and children seldom visit.

The men live a companionable life, sharing their food, eating and relaxing together. A pot of fish stew simmers over the camp fire. Sahat kneels in a corner, facing Mecca, and prays. Ron walks slowly over Em's back to massage his painful muscles. Ip mimics Em nervously crossing a span of bamboos. The men laugh loudly. Their sense of humour and practical jokes make it difficult to believe that they are involved in such dangerous work. Outside the cosy circle of fire-light, an inky blackness has descended. The lapping of waves is a soothing lullaby. A gentle breeze stirs the warm air.

One night the blast of a boat horn disturbs the calm. Ip grabs a walkie-talkie. It crackles for a moment and then a voice speaks. The leaseholder of the caves, Mr Apichat, is approaching on his weekly visit to weigh and collect the nests. The men stand respectfully as Mr Apichat enters the camp accompanied by two armed guards. His round face is wreathed in smiles as he distributes a few gifts: cakes, sweets and soft drinks. He looks much younger than his forty-nine years. His black hair is neatly combed and he is dressed in a spotless white shirt and shorts. On his chest he wears a fine gold chain with a cluster of small talismans.

Mr Apichat brings his men news and mail from home. He knows all the one hundred employees working on his seventy islands personally. He takes care of his men as if they were his own family. Four generations of nest gatherers have worked for Mr Apichat and his forefathers. There is a bond of mutual trust between Mr Apichat and his men. He knows the risks they take to collect the nests. When a new cave is discovered, he climbs with them. When there are new vines and bamboos to replace, he works with them.

In the glare of a petrol lamp, Mr Apichat carefully inspects the week's harvest, while the men look on silently. He weighs the nests on a shiny chrome scale. All eyes watch the needle: 25 kilos of top-quality white nests. Mr Apichat nods his head appreciatively. The men smile.

Two kinds of birds' nests are taken: the white nest of pure saliva built by *A.fuciphagus* and the black nest of *A.maximus*, which incorporates the bird's feathers. The black nest is less valuable because of its impurities. The thorough cleaning process it has to undergo spoils the delicate shape of the nest and results in a smaller amount of edible matter. Less common is the red nest, which is regarded as a great delicacy. Many believe that the red nest is tinted by the blood of the swiftlets who, having exhausted their saliva in building their first two nests, strain to weave the last. In fact, the colour may actually be derived from iron oxide in the rock to which it is attached.

Mr Apichat joins his men for a meal. His short, stocky figure and pale skin denoting his Chinese ancestry contrasts with his slim, dark workers. He is a Buddhist. His employees, like most of the people in this region, are Muslims, the descendants of Malay fishermen.

After dinner, Mr Apichat leaves with the nests and his bodyguards for the journey back to his home on a nearby island. Armed guards must escort the nests on the voyage because thieves sometimes attack the boat. These robbers have guns and do not hesitate to shoot. But as the islands are far away from police posts, Mr Apichat and his men are allowed by law to keep weapons to protect the caves and the boats that carry the 'white gold'.

The harvesting of birds' nests has been big business for hundreds of years. However, the origins of the trade are shrouded in mystery. A leading authority on the history and chemistry of birds' nests, Yun-Cheung Kong, Professor of Biochemistry at the Chinese University of Hong Kong, believes that swiftlets' nests have been eaten in China for 1,500 years. According to Dr Kong, once local supplies had been exhausted, China looked elsewhere for the nests. The discovery of Tang dynasty porcelain, which was traditionally traded for nests, near Niah Cave in north-western Borneo suggests that the importation of the delicacy goes back as far as 700 AD.

Early in the Ming dynasty (1368-1644) a famous Chinese admiral named Cheng Ho made seven voyages throughout South East Asia in command of the 'treasure ships', an armada of hundreds of ships and thousands of men, to make a survey of lands to the south.

His instructions from the emperor were to note in particular the diet and produce of these foreign parts. Cheng Ho's route touched the major bird's nest producing sites of today, and it is possible he brought back samples to present to the imperial court. Some authorities credit Cheng Ho with introducing foreign nests into China, though no written records have been discovered to prove the fact.

The demand for birds' nests in Chinese cuisine and pharmacy developed rapidly. By the mid-seventeenth century they were a prized commodity. In the late 1700s 6 tons (four million nests) passed through the Javanese port of Batavia (Jakarta) annually. In southern Thailand an astute Chinese settler, Hao Yieng, recognized the value of the birds' nests that he had seen on two nearby islands. In about 1770 he presented the king with a list of offerings that included fifty cases of tobacco, his land, wife, children and slaves and begged the king to grant him the right to collect the nests. The king accepted the tobacco, returned the list of people and property and granted Hao Yieng a lease in return for an annual payment.

Until the Communist revolution the biggest importer of birds' nests was China. Today Hong Kong is the largest world market and biggest consumer. Thailand's nests are renowned for their quality. Others are imported from Indonesia, Vietnam, Malaysia, Sabah, Singapore, Sarawak, Vietnam and Burma. Hong Kong consumes about one hundred tons, or twenty-five million dollars' worth, annually. The Chinese communities of North America rank second, accounting for the importation of about 30 tons yearly. The United States does not import the raw nests because of the presence of the bacteria *clostridium*. All nests destined for the North American market are washed in a sulphite solution and cleaned of impurities before export.

The delicacy is mostly eaten at home, but bird's nest soup can also be consumed in Hong Kong restaurants for as much as US $50 for a single bowl. The standard method of preparation is to soak the nests first. The filaments swell to the consistency of a fine noodle and any impurities are removed with tweezers before being cooked in a chicken broth or blended with coconut milk as a dessert. More elegant recipes include 'Phoenix Swallowing the Swallow', a chicken filled with birds' nests and double-boiled in a porcelain pot to yield a clear consommé.

'We eat bird's nest soup as many times as we can afford it,' Dr Kong explained over tea in his laboratory. For centuries the Chinese have given their children bird's nest soup in the belief that it will help them grow.

Others take it regularly to improve their complexion. Sufferers of lung complaints, convalescents and the elderly eat birds' nests as a tonic. 'There's a large amount of truth in the old Chinese beliefs,' Dr Kong says. As part of his research into Chinese herbal and animal medicines, Dr Kong has found that the nests contain a water-soluble glyco-protein that is believed to promote cell division within the immune system.

'If we can manage to isolate this active ingredient known as a mitogen and identify its target cells, it's conceivable that it might be used as an adjunct to the drug AZT to combat the immunodeficiency in AIDS,' Dr Kong speculates.

'Unfortunately the Chinese eat birds' nests only for their texture and out of vanity,' he continues. The water-soluble protein is destroyed in the cleaning process and the valuable properties are thrown out with the water. This is particularly true of the black nests which require exhaustive soaking to remove impurities.

Supplies of birds' nests diminish but demand remains strong. Prices double every two years. Some scientists are concerned that over-harvesting is taking an excessive toll on eggs and young birds. Dr Kong is among them: 'If harvesting continues on this scale, the species may die out before we know what good their nests could do us.'

At the National University of Singapore, the zoology department has been researching harvest-management methods. Dr Kang Nee, who conducted the study, recommends limiting each year's harvest according to the season and the birds' breeding behaviour.

Any harvest-management plan requires the co-operation of cave owners, who would have to accept a short-term reduction in profits in return for a future increase in nest yields.

Mr Apichat is concerned about conservation. The decline of the forests where the birds feed also threatens the nest gatherers' way of life. On the cliffs many rotting bamboos lead to caves once visited by the nest gatherers. They testify to the abundance of nests that were collected there. Now these caves are abandoned and the swiftlets are gone.

'There are no birds left up there,' Ip said, pointing. 'They never came back. But we will follow them. Wherever the birds fly we go.'

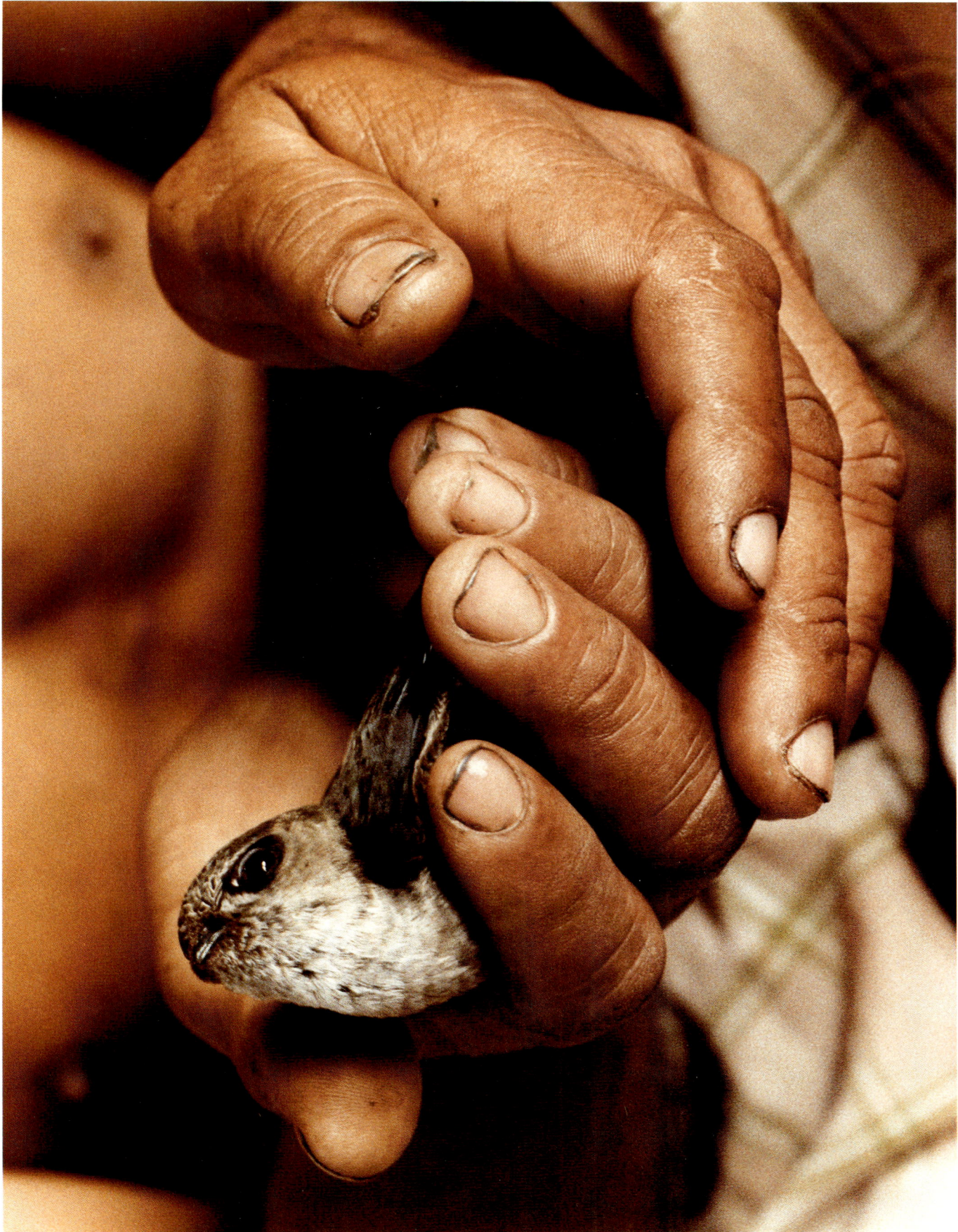

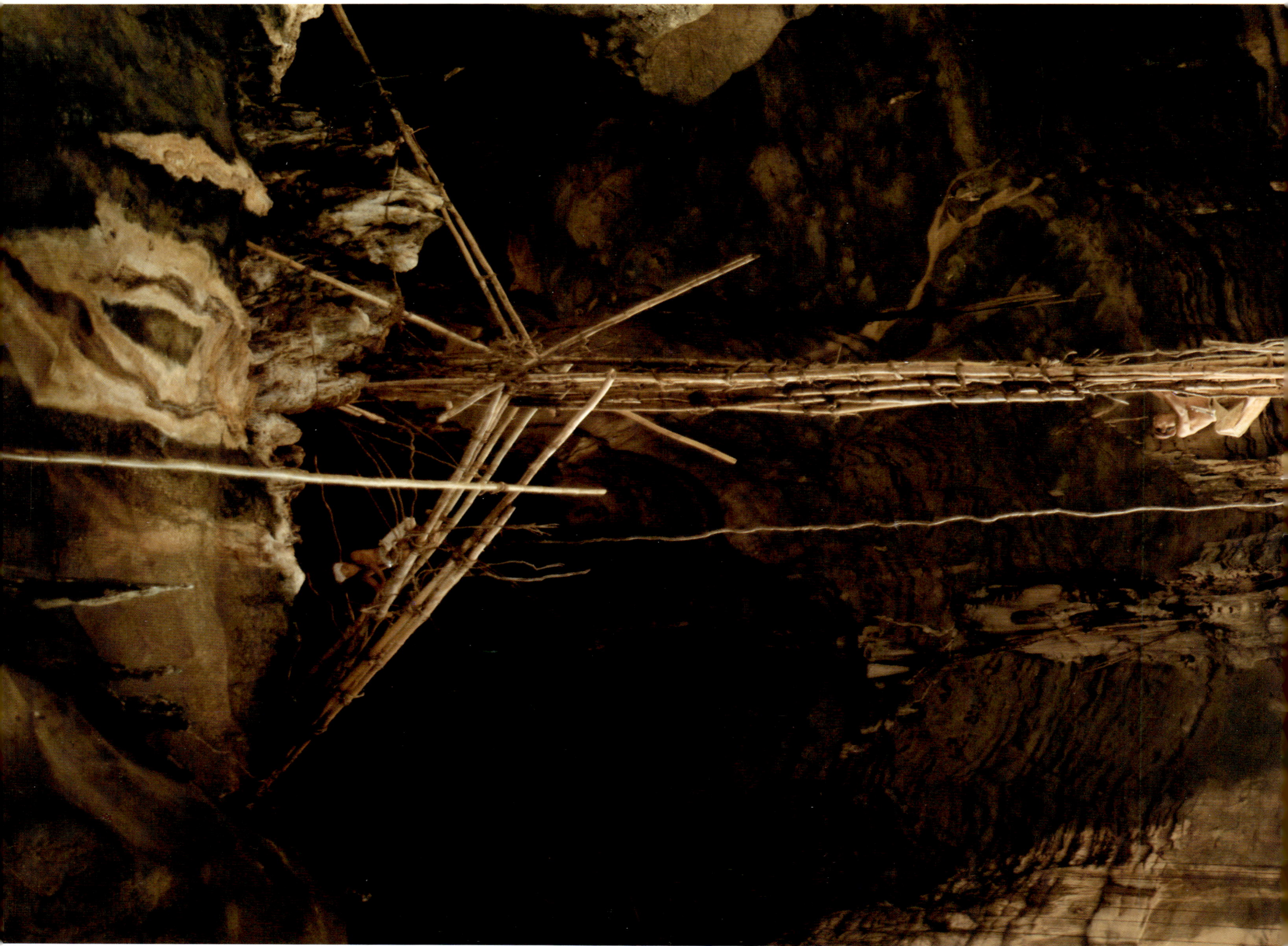

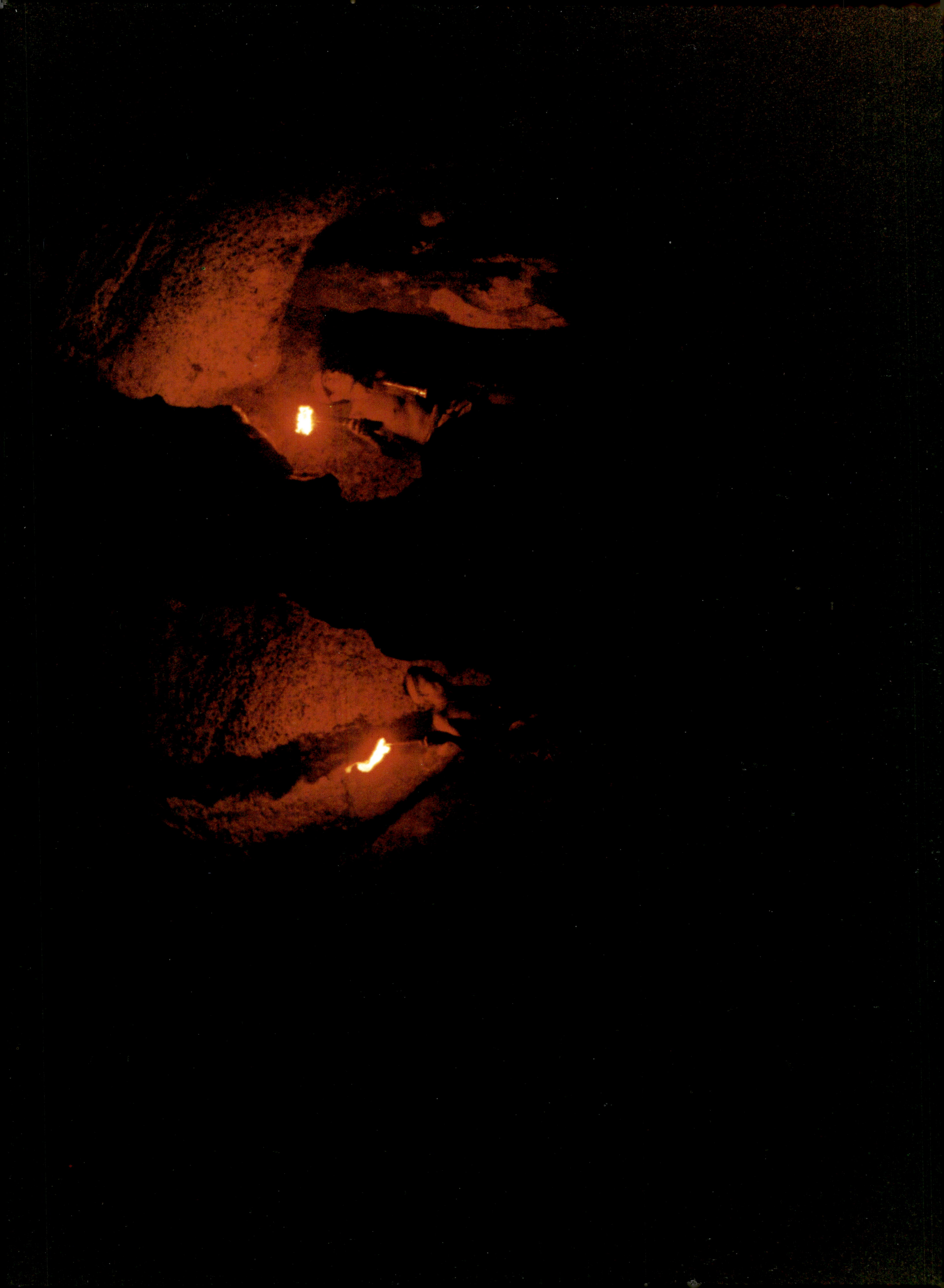

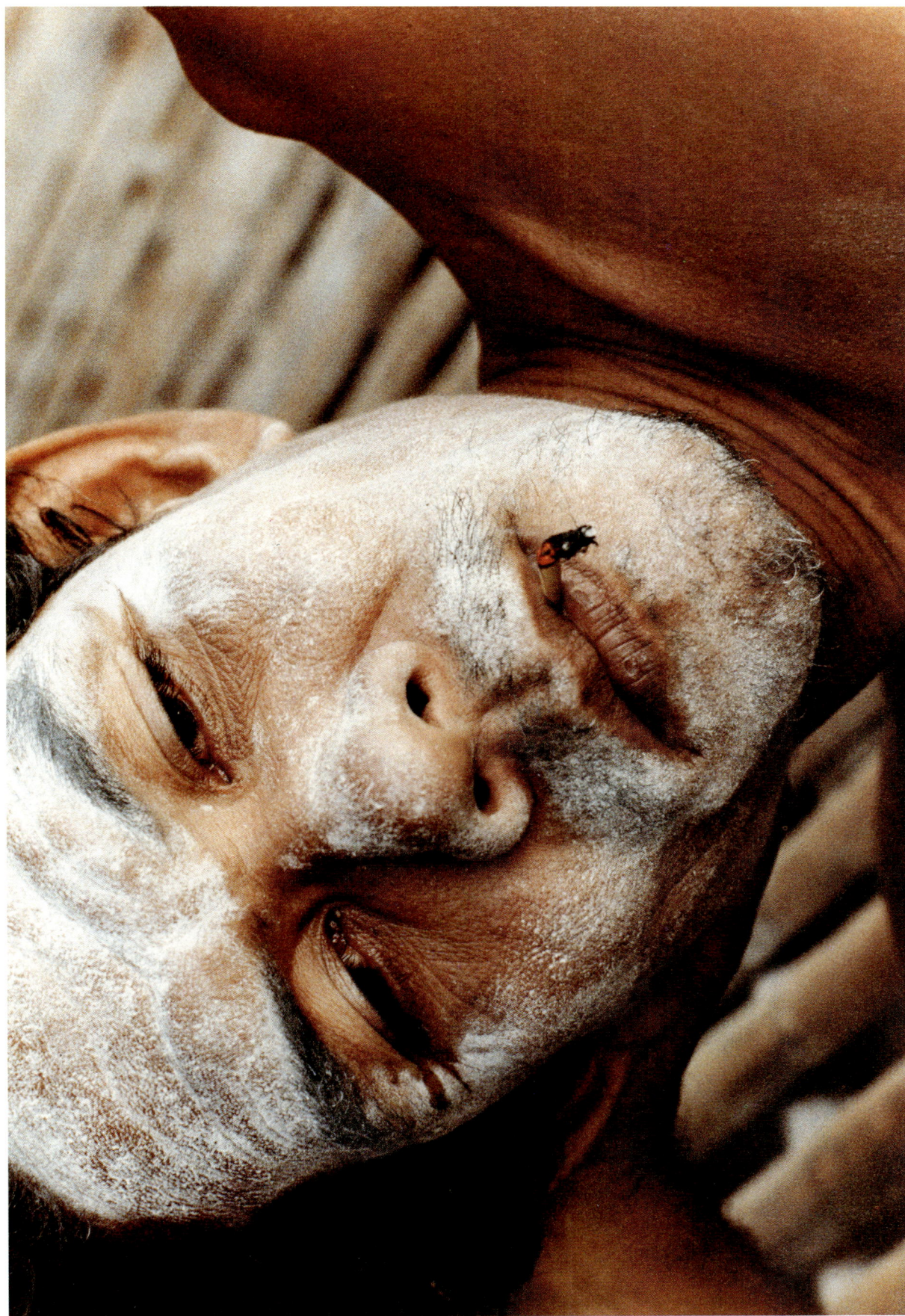

A

B

A. In a Chinese pharmacy in Hong Kong, a shop owner weighs the ingredients for a prescription. As well as being a delicacy, birds' nests are prescribed as a tonic for convalescents and sufferers of lung complaints. Behind him are glass jars containing a variety of nests from different sources – the white, pure-saliva nests of Vietnam and Thailand fetch the highest prices. Less expensive are the black nests which contain more impurities. Rarest of all are the so-called 'red' nests, whose colour probably originates from iron oxide in the rock.

B. Birds' nests are prepared for the table by a thorough soaking in water. Any impurities are removed from the swollen filaments with tweezers. After soaking, the nests resemble fine gelatinous noodles. Birds' nests are a popular delicacy and an essential dish at any Chinese banquet. They can be cooked in a number of ways, the most well known being to blend the nests with chicken stock and fragrant spices to make the famous bird's nest soup.

C

D

C. Hong Kong is the international market for birds' nests. About 60 per cent of the world's supply is consumed there. The rest is exported to Chinese communities all over the globe. In the backrooms of a wholesaler's shop, workers wash black nests to remove the feathers.

D. Suspected thieves, attracted by big profits on the black market for the nests, face two years in jail if convicted.

E

E. Born in the darkness, these young swiftlets will not see light until they are mature enough to fly out of the cave. Their nest is the third built by the parents, the first two having been removed by the nest gatherers before any eggs were laid. The third nest is left for the swiftlets to raise their young and is not taken until after the birds have flown.

In Langsian Cave Ip removes nests hidden in the folds of stalactites. To reach them, he has secured his *rada* and torch to the end of a long bamboo pole. Sahat looks on, directing his companion. The white stains on the rocks in the foreground are caused by spiders.

The lofty vaults of Rimau Cave soar 100 metres high. Ip, on the central pillar, climbs the frail line of bamboos to reach the valuable nests.

Before beginning their dangerous work, Sahat and Ip leave tobacco and coconut milk at the base of a ribboned stalagmite which symbolizes Tok Rimau, the god of the cave. Bamboo pillars lead to the heights.

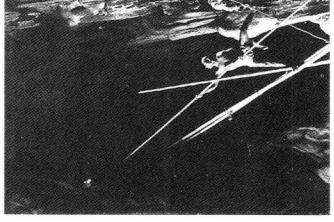

The work of the nest gatherers is strenuous and risky. With one foot balanced on a bamboo and the other on a rock, Ip stretches out with a long pole to pluck the nests from between the folds of rock.

Before starting the difficult and dangerous ascent to the giant stalactite called 'Naked Bottom', Ip prepares the vines on which he will climb.

Ip looks up at Sahat. The older man has discovered a cluster of nests by the light of his torch.

Ip climbs the central pillar. The sheer size of the cave is revealed by the small boat on the cave floor. Erosion has pitted the cave floor like the surface of the moon.

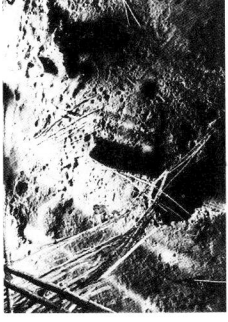

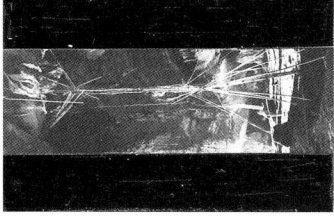

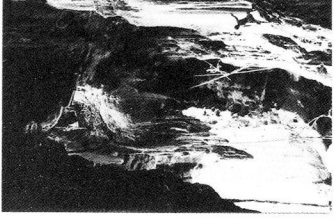

Squatting on a long root dangling down into a chamber, Sahat contemplates the world of darkness into which the nest gatherers venture.

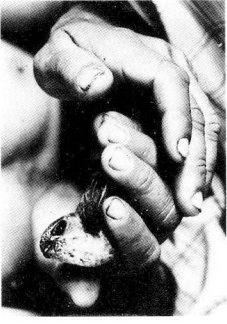

Stunned by the impact, a black-nest swiftlet (*Aerodramus maximus*) rests in Ip's hands after colliding with him in the darkness.

Bamboos cut from jungles on distant islands are brought to the swiftlets' caves to repair the huge scaffolding.

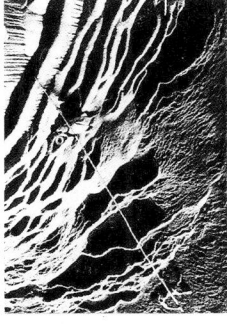

Ip and Em carry a bamboo across a petrified cascade.

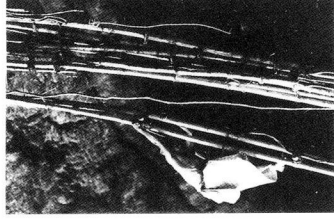

In Rimau Cave Ip climbs a 30-metre-high central pillar known as Chek Dang to reach the network of bamboos woven in the chamber.

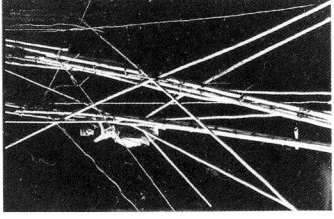

A 12-metre-long mural of ships discovered on the wall of Wong Lung Cave depicts a Chinese vessel (centre) surrounded by others of a Portuguese design. The accurate detail suggests that the artists were sailors who visited the islands to collect the nests.
Birds' nests and other goods were once carried by elephants (bottom left) across the jungle and traded with the Chinese for *celadon*, a highly prized pottery.

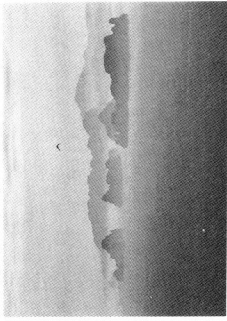

On weather-worn islands of the Saka archipelago, swiftlets build their nests in sea caves, some as large as cathedrals. In the early morning, two birds cross the sky on their way to forage for insects living in the forests.

A nest gatherer enters a sea cavern, its entrance silhouetted against the sky. Another man, on guard against thieves who come to steal the valuable nests, looks out from a watch post.

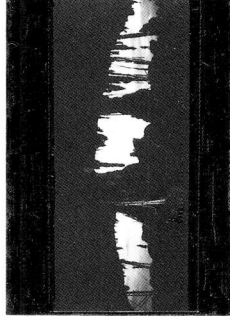

The yawning entrance to Rimau, the Tiger Cave. Stalactites, stalagmites and pillars of bamboo frame the mouth of the cavern.

From their boat anchored in the bay of Chang Luk Cave, the nest gatherers have hooked a 15-metre-long bamboo pole on to the rock. Taking care not to pull the pole off its precarious grip, a nest gatherer named Samane pulls himself gingerly towards the cave opening high above the sea.

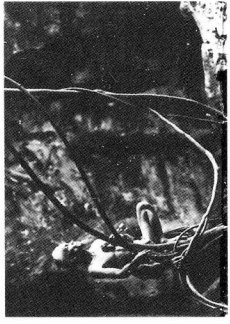

Ip greets a passing fishing boat from the mouth of Lo Liam Cave in the Saka archipelago. The opening of the cave lies 15 metres above the sea.

To protect their valuable harvest from thieves, nest gatherers are often heavily armed.

During the harvest season home is a bamboo platform suspended by vines from the cave roof. Half a dozen climbers of Taluk Cave share living quarters.
Each man has a sleeping area, shielded by a screen and sometimes decorated by a pin-up. A boy watches his father calculate the week's harvest. Karia, a retired nest gatherer and the cook, prepares fish for dinner.

Agile as a monkey, Samane shins up the bamboo pole leading to the entrance of Chang Luk Cave. His companions have moved the boat to one side in case he falls.

Ip returns from fishing to collect Sahat from a cave. Sahat passes him a bag containing the day's harvest.

High on a tiny rock platform, Ip and Sahat examine the day's harvest before descending.
To the left vines are secured to the rock in a knot called Hua Dao, a sacred place believed to be inhabited by the gods.

After a long day on the bamboo web, the climbers descend.

Covered with dirt and guano, the men bathe in the sea.

After washing, the men powder their faces with talc.

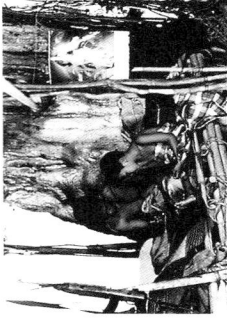

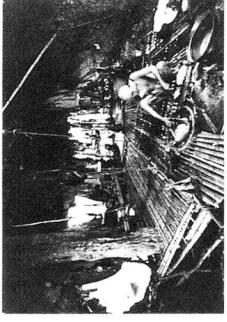

By torchlight Ip and Sahat follow a tunnel leading deep inside the bowels of the earth.

Where the rocks are too wet and the scaffolding rots quickly, the climbers use a 'walking bamboo' to reach the nests. Like the lookout perched on a ship's mast, Ip sits on top of a long bamboo guyed by vines. From this vantage point he removes the nests. When he has finished, he signals to his companions below to move the 'walking bamboo' to the next wall. (Photograph copyright National Geographic Society)

Ip, Sahat and Em penetrate the darkness of a hidden chamber in Rimau Cave.

To keep his hands free, Sahat grips a torch between his teeth as he searches for nests. These torches are made from bark soaked in resinous sap and tied with string. They cast a broad light which is more useful than the narrow beams of the climbers' flashlights.

Ip and Sahat harvest a nest in the limestone cascade.

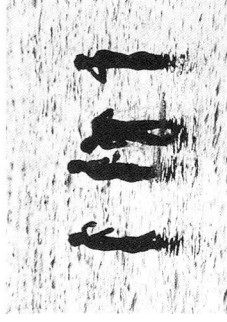

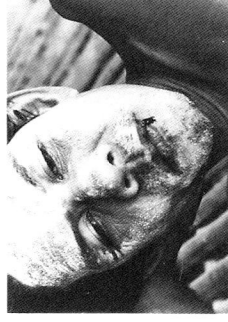

The nest gatherers usually climb on the bamboo and vine scaffolding built by man. But in Langsiam Cave the strong roots hanging down from the top of the chamber provide a rope.

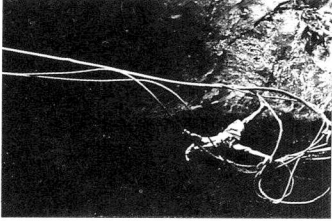

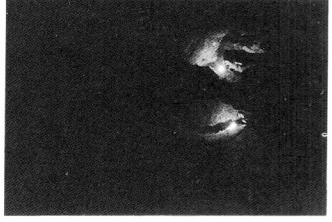

A team of nest gatherers led by Ron (second from the right) pose at Khalad Island.

Sahat and Em with their families and Ip pictured at the foot of bamboo pillars.

Ip stretches out to pluck white nests from the cave wall. Rotten bamboos covering the cave floor testify to the generations that have been erecting the scaffolding.

With nothing but skill to keep him from falling, Sahat reaches out from the bamboo scaffolding to pluck a bird's nest from the cave wall with his *rada*. (Photograph copyright National Geographic Society)

In one hand Sahat holds the tool of his craft, the *rada*, which is thought to possess magical powers. White nests shine in the other.

Within grasp of the precious 'white gold', Sahat wedges himself into the folds of a stalactite and reaches up with his *rada*. His bag is secured to his belt.

Sahat carries a bundle of vines called *chekra* to tie the bamboos together.

Halfway up Ke Rua, the 'Pillar of the Boat', Em and Sahat cross a bamboo bridge secured to a stalactite by vines. The climb does not allow for any errors. Below is a drop of 50 metres.

As they approach the top of the chamber, Ip and Sahat strengthen the bamboo scaffolding with vines. Their lives depend on the safety of the structure.

Like a gigantic spiderweb, the fantastic bamboo walkway covers the 90-metre-high walls of Rimau Cave's main chamber. The torches of the four climbers cast pinpricks of light in the dark.
To the left, at the top of the chamber, the rock face is dotted with tiny black nests.

Clinging to bundles of vines that have been lashed to 'Naked Bottom', Sahat, his son Em, and his companion Ip, use torches to search for nests. Em stretches over to take a cluster of nests under the guidance of his father. 25 metres below a man stands on the cave floor.

Ip and Sahat scour the cave walls for nests.

This panoramic view shows four men scaling a pylon called Lumu or 'Pierced Nose'. The pylon leads straight up to a nostril-like hole through which vines are threaded to secure the bamboo to the rock face. From there the men continue to climb up a series of stalactites on yet more vines and bamboos to a height of 80 metres.

Ip climbs vines covering the stalactite called 'Naked Bottom' to join Sahat.